Manag

Planning

Kate Keenan

RAVETTE BOOKS

Published by Ravette Books Limited
P.O. Box 296
Horsham
West Sussex RH13 8FH
Tel & Fax: (01 403) 711443

Series Editor – Anne Tauté
Editor – Catriona Scott

Cover design – Jim Wire
Printing & Binding – Cox & Wyman Ltd.
Production – Oval Projects Ltd.

An Oval Project
produced for Ravette Books.

Cover – Finding a way through the
labyrinth is made a good deal easier
by working to a plan.

Acknowledgments and thanks to:
Barry Tuckwood
Jeremy Bethell

Contents

This book is dedicated to
those who would like to manage better
but are too busy to begin.

Planning

Being successful does not usually happen by accident. It is generally acknowledged that following an overall plan plays a large part.

Planning is the activity which gets you from where you are now to where you want to be. It consists of analysing your current situation, deciding on your objectives and plotting your action.

Unfortunately, people rarely find enough time to think about or plan for the future. They will tell you that what happens day-to-day takes up so much of their time, there is no time left for planning.

But thinking about your ultimate aim is vital if you are to achieve what you want. This book shows you how to get to grips with planning and offers some effective ways to get you started.

1.   The Need to Plan

Planning involves taking a systematic approach to what you are doing. For many people this is simply too difficult. "Things are always changing so it's not worth planning" is the constant refrain.

It is true that change is an ever-present factor. Indeed, change is necessary for progress to take place. However, if you make no attempt to plan, in the belief that it is not worth the effort, you will be even less in control than you are now.

Busy Being Busy

When you are very busy, it is easy to convince yourself that getting on with the job is your first priority and that having a plan is an optional extra which you might get around to at some time or another.

This excuse for not planning may be covering other fundamental reasons why you are not prepared to take the idea of planning seriously. For example you may be:

- Lacking the confidence or knowledge as to how to start the planning process.
- Feeling intimidated by the commitment which planning requires.
- Thinking that planning will use precious time which could be better spent on meeting deadlines.

It could be that you have not fully appreciated the difference between movement and action and how this relates to planning. **Movement** is when you respond to things as they crop up, often unexpectedly, and work hard to overcome them. These usually come in the form of crises which must be resolved immediately. **Action** is purposeful and comes about when you have thought things through and anticipated what needs to be done.

It is essential you do not confuse doing work with producing results. Most people find that 80% of their time only produces 20% of the results. The aim is to reverse these percentages. Working through the planning process plays a major part in achieving a better level of efficiency.

The fact is that without a plan you usually end up just busy being busy. This means that things either happen of their own accord or opportunities are missed. Either way, you are not in control and the situation can only drift on or get worse.

Managing Functions

Managing anything properly involves carrying out four major functions, preferably in this order:

- Identifying what you want to achieve – planning.
- Putting your plans into practice – organizing.

- Telling others what to do – directing.
- Ensuring that things have been done and to the right standard – controlling.

If these activities are not carried out in this order, you may by-pass the planning function because you think you know already what it is you want to achieve. You may well be moving straight into the more concrete and visible activities of organizing, directing and controlling. Each of these three functions is important, but if planning is neglected, you are unlikely to carry them out effectively because you are not sure what your overall aims are.

Planning acts as the cornerstone to the others, for without a firm grasp of what it is you want to achieve, all other activity could be a waste of effort.

Good Intentions

It is easy to be put off by the thought of planning and what this entails. Often this is because you are unsure about what you have to do or fear that it entails complex procedures. For example:

- Suppose you always had an ambition to have a book published, how do you go about achieving it?
- Or, suppose you run a travel agency and are doing reasonably well but know you could be doing better, how do you do so?

What it boils down to is that people often think planning is too difficult, so they never begin. It is all very well to have the intention to do something but it is often more difficult to get going and do it. The relationship between your intentions and what you actually do is not always straightforward. Many external factors can prevent the best of intentions from becoming actions.

In general, your intentions are more likely to become actions if you take a positive and resolute approach to the planning process. The most important thing, therefore, is your commitment to making a plan.

Summary: Getting Started

Get rid of all your preconceived ideas about planning. Make your mind a blank. Now ask yourself these four questions:

- Where am I now?

- Where do I want to be?

- How will I get there?

- How will I know when I have got there?

This is all that planning is about.

Questions to Ask Yourself

Think about your attitude to planning and answer these questions:

➤ Have I ever said, "I haven't got time to plan"?

➤ Do I tend to spend my time managing crises rather than getting things done?

➤ Have I missed opportunities due to lack of planning?

➤ Does the thought of planning put me off?

➤ Do I have lots of good intentions, but find it difficult to organize the action?

➤ Do I suspect that planning would make a difference to my effectiveness?

If you have answered 'Yes' to some or all of these questions, it is high time you gave some attention to planning.

You Will Be Doing Better If...

★ You realize that you have been procrastinating for far too long.

★ You know you should be doing as much planning as you are organizing, directing and controlling.

★ You are resolved to make your intentions become a reality.

★ You are no longer intimidated by the thought of planning.

★ You are prepared to set some time aside to plan.

2. Taking Stock

Assessing your current situation ('Where am I now?') is the first and most essential step in planning. Knowing where you are starting from makes it very much easier to determine where you want to be.

If you don't know where you are going, you usually arrive somewhere else. This is especially true if you have not analysed the current situation. The best way to do this is to take a 'snapshot' of it.

The Snapshot

The purpose of this is to gain an accurate picture of how things are performing. An analysis of what is happening will provide you with a solid basis from which to project into the future. You need to assess these four aspects:

- **The strong points** – those talents you have and what works well in the business.

- **The weak spots** – those things you can and need to improve; or those you cannot and need to avoid.

- **The opportunities** – those areas where there are or could be chances for you, either in your current sphere of activity or outside it.

- **The threats** – those obstacles which could prevent you from doing what you want to do.

This will reveal the good, the bad and the ugly about yourself and your business.

Strong Points

By identifying your strong points you gain a level of confidence which will prove vital when other things may not be going quite as well as planned. "Well, at least I'm good at ..."

By definition, strengths reflect those aspects where performance is good, for example your own personal skills and abilities, the talents of those who work with you and the business advantages you may have.

Identifying these strong points is not always easy. People are often diffident about 'blowing their own trumpet'. However, if strengths are not realistically identified, the plan you formulate may not accurately reflect your potential or that of the business. After all, if you don't blow your own trumpet, it can never play your tune.

The secret is to write down everything you can think of about yourself and your organization which could be considered an asset.

Make a list under two headings:

1. **My/Our Strong Points** – that is, your own (and other people's).

2. **The Company's Strong Points** – those of your business or profession.

Your list could include:

- The technical abilities and skills that you (or others) have.

- The quality of your product or service e.g. well-designed, customer-friendly.

- Your own and other people's understanding of the business and its possibilities.

- A good physical location or work environment.

- Positive attitudes towards getting things done.

- The level of commitment to what you are doing and to that of the business.

- The working atmosphere, e.g. contented, productive.

When completed, you will find that either your own strengths or those of the business are generally better than you thought – possibly both. This will enable you to understand your advantages. It may even help you realize you have a great deal to be proud of.

Weak Spots

These are things that you would really rather not know, but which, fortunately, are usually easy to identify. They relate to areas where you could and should be doing better.

As before, make two lists of those things where performance, both your own and other people's, is not achieving what is required and where your business is not doing well.

It can be depressing to dwell on shortcomings, but understanding where things need improvement is important. Indeed, knowing your weaknesses is at least as important as knowing your strengths. It enables you to see what needs attention, such as:

- Being disorganized and therefore giving an impression of not being in control.

- Taking on too much without sufficient resources to ensure successful completion.

- Promising things in an impossible time-scale and then not delivering.

- Not admitting that there are things you cannot do.

Recognizing the weak spots is the first step towards improving your performance. Acknowledging your limitations also prevents you from trying to achieve things which you should never have attempted in the first place.

Opportunities

Having looked inwards, the next step is to look outwards at what could affect you or your business, and to work out how external opportunities could develop your activities in ways you had not previously considered. For example, think about:

- Trends in your business: new markets, perhaps abroad – how could they open up opportunities for you?

- Developments in technology: the latest advances in computers and communications – how could these be of benefit to you?

- Changes in national policies: health, environment, re-cycling – how might you be able to use these to your advantage?

- Movements in social patterns: population changes, recreational developments – how could you use such things to do more business?

Think about what you could do in the future to capitalize on any of these opportunities. The answers may not be obvious and may even require some lateral thinking. Try exploring your options in a creative way and making connections which are not always evident.

Identifying your opportunities helps you assess how your strengths could be further developed and used more profitably. Exploring new directions ensures that you are looking beyond your immediate situation and are keeping abreast of changes and trends.

Threats

Nobody likes to think about what horrors might be waiting in the wings. But it is important when taking stock of your situation that you face up to possibilities, such as:

- New and/or existing competition.

- Changing requirements.

- Bad debts or cash flow problems.

If you confront your worst fears, you will be less beset by uncertainty which, of itself, can prevent you from taking action.

By considering the obstacles, you will probably find that:

- Your worst scenario is not quite as bad as you first feared.

- You can work out what can be done to solve or prevent a difficult situation.

- You will have a contingency plan, previously prepared for coping, should the worst occur.

Things that threaten always seem worse if not confronted. They lurk in the background and bring a sense of unease and helplessness both of which prevent you from moving forward. By identifying where things could go wrong, you can work out how to react in any given situation. "If I can't prevent that, I'll do this." Having a contingency plan is a form of security blanket. It allows you to feel that all is never totally lost.

Coping with emergencies and crises is not just exhausting but hugely time-consuming. If you have given thought to what might happen, you not only reduce the shock should it do so, but prevent a delay in reacting to it. For example, "If my business fails, I'll realize my remaining assets and move sooner than expected to a bolt-hole in France."

Facing up to the dangers decreases your fear of failure and enables you to take action.

Looking at the Picture

Taking a long, hard look at the snapshot gives you a clear idea of what's what. For example:

As a potential author the snapshot might show:

Strong points: I write well; I have a good imagination, and I have a blockbuster idea.

Weak spots: I am not well organized. The idea has been in my head for the last six years and I have still done nothing about it.

Opportunities: The novel is about foul play amongst athletes which could be published at a peak period of interest such as the European or Olympic Games.

Threats: My elderly parents now need much more attention than before.

As the travel agency, the picture might be:

Strong points: We offer a wide range of services; have a keen, if young, staff; and cheap, well-located premises.

Weak spots: The staff are inexperienced at selling.

Opportunities: The town is growing fast due to a new high-speed train service; excellent sales training schemes are run locally.

Threats: We could be overtaken by competition if we do nothing to distinguish ourselves.

These examples indicate how taking a snapshot can highlight positive areas and indicate opportunities. At the same time, identifying the areas to be improved or where dangers may lurk ensures a balanced approach.

Summary: Where I Am Now

The information obtained when conducting your analysis lets you know where your strong points lie. It also highlights the weak spots you may need to sort out before doing anything else.

Identifying the current situation focuses your attention on the issues which will be vital to your success.

At some point, however, you have to stop and get on with the next stage. Planning requires a sense of urgency if you are to keep up with things and stay ahead. Beware of 'paralysis by analysis', which is the downside of conducting any review.

So if analysing your current situation indicates that there is a hole in your bucket, then fix it. On the other hand, if you are reasonably content with the status quo, you are ready to move on and make plans to realize your aims.

Questions to Ask Yourself

Think about your current situation and answer the following questions.

➤ Have I identified my strong points and those of others involved?

➤ Do I know the strong points of the business?

➤ Am I aware of my own weak spots and those of others?

➤ Am I aware of the weak spots of the business?

➤ Have I considered what opportunities are available to me and to the business?

➤ Have I given any thought to any pitfalls which could arise?

➤ Have I worked out how I might be able to cope with the worst possible scenario?

➤ Have I a clear picture of the current situation?

You Will Be Doing Better If...

★ You know what you are good at and what your business does well.

★ You know what you do not do well.

★ You know the areas that need improving in the business.

★ You work out where your opportunities lie.

★ You envisage the ominous things that might materialize and prevent you from achieving your goals.

★ You draw up some contingency plans to meet the worst of your fears.

★ You have a clear and accurate picture of your current situation.

3. Defining the Aims

Planning is about looking into the future and deciding what you want ('Where do I want to be?'). But it is not something you can just rush out and do. It is very important to establish the right direction to take.

To know where you want to go, the first step is to be sure you know what business you are in. This is not always as obvious as it seems. What you produce or the service you provide may not always accurately reflect the market in which you are operating. For instance, if you run a florist's shop, are you in the horticultural business or the gift business?

The overall aims of the business will be different: if you are in horticulture, you are likely to be more concerned with the variety of the product; if it is the gift business, how your product is packaged and the speed of your service will take priority.

Identifying Your Ultimate Aim

If you throw yourself into your business, without determining specifically what you want to do, you will almost certainly be dissipating your efforts.

Envisaging how you would like the future to develop is an astonishingly effective way to concentrate attention on what you want to achieve.

You do this by defining what your business or profession is all about and where it is going. This is often called a 'vision statement': in fact, it is simply a main purpose, or ultimate aim.

No business is too small to have its own sense of purpose. Defining your ultimate aim is about looking towards the horizon to determine where you really want to be. It should identify the underlying (often altruistic) goals of your business or profession, before indicating the more concrete ones.

For instance, a small delivery business wanting to be a national courier network might have as its ultimate aim:

"To provide a first class service."

The would-be author might have as an ultimate aim:

"To thrill readers worldwide."

And the ultimate aim of the travel agency might be:

"To give people the time of their lives."

To aspire to be simply the best in your field does not comprise an adequate ultimate aim. It leaves too much room for dreaming or wishful thinking instead of being a clear statement of intention. There may also be confusion between the overall purpose and financial goals. For example, "I/We want to make a million dollars" does not constitute an ultimate aim – merely the desirable outcome.

Finding the Way

In order to make your ultimate aim operational, you have to work out the specific goals necessary for achieving it (often referred to as 'mission statements'). To do this, you need to ask the following questions – which will ensure that you head in the right direction:

- **What am I in business for?** (the rationale of your organization or profession, its direction and priorities).

- **What do I believe in?** (the ethics, principles and codes of conduct governing the activities of the business).

- **What standards am I aiming for?** (the areas of excellence critical to the business).

- **What return do I seek?** (the expected outcome from the efforts expended).

The answers to these issues usually require a fair amount of thought and often some soul-searching.

Writing down the answers is a practical starting point for determining the actions which you and your business will take. They will ensure that the activities which form your detailed plan will lead you towards your ultimate aim.

Involving Others

Your ultimate aim also has to be communicated to everyone involved. Unless there is a clear and shared concept of, and commitment to, what is to be achieved, the chances of everyone pulling in the same direction are minimal. By involving those concerned, you gain a willing and committed group of people who are as enthusiastic as you are about your plans.

To find out how others are thinking about the future, you need to ask these questions:

- How is the future of the business viewed: "Where do you think we ought to be going?"

- What is the potential of the business: "What do you think we could be doing?"

- What should be the overall objectives: "Whatever the current position, what would you like us to be achieving?"

The answers to these questions are usually quite revealing. Unfortunately, people do not always have a vision for the future of the business other than assuming that it will probably continue as it always has. This is not very helpful. If you are not doing very well at something, doing more of the same will almost certainly not improve the situation.

The difference in people's perceptions may well be substantial. If you do not have a united view of the future, success will be more difficult, if not impossible, to achieve. It means the answer to the question, "Where do we want to be?" may have wide variations.

Holding discussions with the people involved will explore any lack of agreement in the way the future is viewed. By asking people to think about the overall goals of the business, they become more aware of the underlying purpose. Plans tend to work better when those involved in implementing them have been consulted or at least informed about the role they are required to play.

To make your ultimate aim work, it is essential that everyone:

- Wants it to happen.
- Believes it will happen.
- Is totally committed to making it happen and will not be deterred by setbacks.
- Communicates that belief and commitment to others.

Making sure everyone is fully aware of what they are expected to do and why, enables them to play a full part in achieving the ultimate aim. Without this commitment, plans will be more difficult to implement; with it, your success is far more likely.

Summary: Where I Want to Be

Your ultimate aim acts as a lodestar when determining your overall direction. It also determines the fundamental values which underpin the actions you take to achieve your more specific goals. Working these out and writing them down is a positive act which gets you underway.

Your ultimate aim helps you to keep your eyes firmly fixed on the horizon so that you start off on the right path. It is the guiding light for all your activities.

It is important that you involve any other people concerned early on in this process as it ensures that they are fully informed about the direction of the business and it gives them an opportunity to make a contribution.

When the going gets tough, being able to remind yourself and others of where you ultimately want to be gives you a fixed focus and provides a degree of certainty in an otherwise uncertain world.

Questions to Ask Yourself

Think about defining your purpose and answer the following questions:

➤ Have I decided what business I am in?

➤ Have I worked out the ultimate aim of the business?

➤ Do I know what I am in business for?

➤ Have I identified the principles by which the business will be run?

➤ Have I specified the desired standards of excellence for the business?

➤ Have I calculated the returns expected from all the blood, sweat and tears?

➤ Have I asked others for their ideas?

➤ Have I written down the ultimate aim?

➤ Have I made sure that everyone concerned believes in the ultimate aim?

You Will Be Doing Better If...

★ You answer the question, "What business am I in?" without hesitation.

★ You identify your ultimate aim.

★ You are clear about the rationale which directs your business.

★ You spell out the values which underpin all your activities.

★ You know what quality of service or product you need to achieve to ensure success.

★ You work out the return you expect from your efforts.

★ You consult with everyone concerned when formulating the ultimate aim.

★ You write down the ultimate aim.

★ Everyone is totally committed to the same aim.

4.   Planning the Detail

Knowing where you are going in overall terms does not tell you how you are going to get there. Your ambition may be to become a famous author because you know you have an important novel in you, or it may be to become the best travel agency in town because you are convinced you can offer the best service – but you need a detailed plan to make it happen ('How will I get there?').

Putting plans into practice can often appear difficult and demanding. Most plans look daunting because of their size and complexity. But if you break down your plan into separate stages the whole thing will become much easier to tackle.

Identifying Key Activities

In order to make your plan operational, you need to generate a list of the important stages, or key activities, of what must be done to achieve it.

So, if your aim is to be a world-famous author, your list of key activities might look something like this:

1. Write an outline and sample chapter.
2. Find a publisher.
3. Make time for completing the book in six months.

And if you want to widen your travel business to include profitable luxury holidays your list of key activities could look like this:

1. Find out about the market.
2. Identify and sell appropriate products.
3. Ensure personal service.
4. Train the staff in sales skills.
5. Promote the agency to attract new customers.

It is important that, having decided on your key activities, you commit them to paper. If you do not have a record of the precise things you need to do, you will almost certainly forget something critical. If you forget to pour the sherry into the trifle, the trifle, for all the effort, will not be the success you hoped for.

However, it is one thing to list the key activities but it is another to make sure they are the right ones. Once you have written them down, check if each is right by asking "Why am I doing this?" until the answer leads back to your ultimate aim.

For instance, the travel agency would ask of their first activity: "Why do we need to find out about the market?" (Answer: To identify the sorts of holidays people wish to enjoy.) "Why are we doing this?" (Answer: So we can offer them what they want.) "Why are we doing this?" (Answer: To give them the time of their lives.)

Planning the Action

To make each of your key activities operational, you need to specify the work involved together with estimates of time and cost. So for each key activity you need to make a separate, detailed plan of action.

Work Involved (How to do it)

Asking yourself "How?" you can achieve each activity will allow you to break things down into specific actions and enable you to generate ideas on how these can be achieved.

For example:

For the author:

Key activity number 2 is to find a publisher. To do this, publishers who might be interested in publishing the work need to be identified. Thus:

a. Visit library to find books of similar genre and see who publishes them.
b. Check the names with a directory of publishers which lists their publishing interests.
c. Draw up a list of suitable names and addresses.

Then a similar list of work needs to be compiled in order to accomplish key activities 1 and 3.

For the travel agency:

Key activity number 1 is to find out about the market. To do this the types of people living in the locality and their lifestyle need to be identified. This can be done by:

a. Checking the habits and spending power of people in the area – e.g. talking to local newspaper editors and finding out from estate agents what sort of properties are available, and/or selling.
b. Assessing which destinations are currently fashionable, or likely to become so.
c. Looking back over previous records to see what sorts of holidays have been sold, and to which customers.

Then a list of all the actions needed for key activities 2-4 needs to be drawn up.

Timetable (When it should be done by)

To schedule your key activities, you need to work out roughly when each action can be achieved. When added up these give you an approximate completion date – a mock deadline – for the entire plan, for example, 'By Christmas'. From this estimated target, work backwards through the months and weeks assigning specific dates by which each action needs to be completed and build in some 'contingency' time so that any slight delays do not become major crises. You usually find when you have finished doing this that you should have started yesterday or, preferably, last year.

You will find the process of assigning time-scales to achieving the various plans of action puts some urgency into their execution.

Once you have fixed these dates you can assign a definite target date for completion, e.g. instead of 'By Christmas', the completion date may be 10 January. (Note that it is always longer than you think.)

For example:

For the author:

- Write to three publishers by 21 May.
- Identify six possible publishers by 30 April (three most suitable plus three more as a back-up).
- Complete outline and sample chapter by 1 March.

For the travel agency:

- Hold a promotional evening for luxury cruises on 31 January.
- Complete catering arrangements by 14 January.
- Send out invitations on 28 December.
- Compile an invitation list of potential and existing clients by 1 December.
- Make provisional booking of venue on 1 November.

Costs (How much it will be)

Setting the costs for each key activity is an important part of planning. When added up, these will produce a total which forms an overall budget – the amount of money you require to implement your plan. You need to question the costs and ensure that items are neither under-estimated nor outrageously expensive – e.g. "How much would it be reasonable to spend on postage and stationery?"

You should also work out what gain is expected from your costs. For example:

For the travel agency, it is important to know that the costs the plan will incur will be out-weighed by the benefits. (For instance: "If we spend £300 on our promotional party, we need to sell a minimum of one cruise in the West Indies at £3,500 per person to gain the 10% commission to cover the cost. If we can't guarantee at least four more people to book it, then it's not worthwhile.")

For the author, there may be some financial costs, but the greatest resource which requires budgeting is likely to be time. ("Can I expect my spouse to take on the dual household responsibilities for six months to give me two hours of uninterrupted writing time every day, so that the revenue from my book can buy us a luxury cruise in the Caribbean?")

Prioritizing

Once you have planned the details of each of your key activities, you need to put them into the right order so that you make sure you will do things in the right sequence. If you do not work out the order in which your actions should be carried out, you may end up working on something which cannot be completed before a more crucial task has been accomplished. This may result in a total waste of time.

Writing the Plan

It is all very well working out how you will achieve your key activities, but you will find it difficult to remember all the things you intend to do if you do not collect your thoughts and write them down. Until you get your ideas on paper, it cannot be designated a plan.

So write down the details of what you intend to do for each key activity, along with the time-scales and costs.

Get it written, even if it is not quite right first time. The plan is a working document. You should expect to go through several drafts before you achieve a satisfactory final version. Indeed if you do not spend time checking and improving, you should question if your initial plan is any good.

It can be a good idea to use different coloured papers for different drafts. Every time you change to a fresh colour, say from green to pink, you know you are nearer to achieving the final version. This way you will not get involved in a paper chase, nor bogged down by messy alterations and lose your way.

To make sure you do not lose valuable bits of information from one draft to another use different symbols to mark the pieces you want to retain or relocate to another section. For example: ✱ ○ ❑ ▲ ① ② ③

When possible, consult with someone else. You not only get a chance to check your own ideas but you may find they have ideas you never thought of.

Summary: How I Will Get There

Spending time on a beautiful plan is all very well but it is a waste of time if you just sit and look at it, or file it, or, worse still, shelve it altogether. Think of it as your guidelines for getting things done.

Committing your plans to paper is the first step in achieving your key activities. It makes your overall aims or ambitions seem that much less abstract and remote.

But making plans is a futile activity without your whole-hearted commitment. You have to be determined to do it, the rest will follow if the will is there.

Questions to Ask Yourself

Think about putting your plan into action and answer the following questions:

➤ Have I identified the key activities I need to carry out in order to achieve my ultimate aim?

➤ Have I worked out the details of what I need to do for each activity?

➤ Have I set realistic dates for key activities, and allowed time for snags and hitches?

➤ Have I estimated the costs and is the overall budget reasonable?

➤ Have I made sure that the action plans for each key activity are in the right order?

➤ Have I written out my plan?

➤ Am I using my plan as my guideline for getting things done and not just for decoration?

You Will Be Doing Better If...

★ You identify your key activities.

★ You make detailed plans of action for each of your key activities.

★ You set a realistic target date for the entire plan, and build in a generous contingency factor to the timetable.

★ You calculate the costs and you feel your budget is sensible.

★ You organize your plans of action in order of priority.

★ You write down all the details and revise and check them thoroughly.

★ You are committed to putting your plan into action.

5.   Carrying out the Action

In order to carry out your plan, you simply start work on your key activities. But to know how you are doing, you need to keep track of progress. This means having a system which allows you to check what has been done and what still needs doing.

It involves:

- Keeping tabs on what is happening on a day-to-day basis to make sure the everything is proceeding according to plan.

- Devising contingency plans should it be necessary to modify the action.

- Acting promptly when you spot something may not be going according to plan in order to get everything back on course.

Monitoring the action is the most important part of the plan, because if you do not know how close you are to achieving your various key activities, you will not know if all your efforts are worthwhile.

It is no good carrying on doing something if there is no chance of it being accomplished. Equally, it is not productive to go on doing something if you have achieved all that you can in the circumstances.

Co-ordinating Activities

You need a way of mapping you actions and checking your progress. From a practical point of view, the simpler the system, the more successful. Two of the most effective methods are a year planner and a diary, both of which enable you to co-ordinate activities without difficulty.

Your year planner can act as a project management chart because you can log key activities on it which show the various tasks, their duration and completion dates. By having a simple visual tracking system, it is clear how the plan is supposed to work out and easy to keep an eye on its progress. Mark important dates with a distinctive sticker to remind you that key things need to be done by then. For example:

For the author the planner could show:

- 'Finish library research – 20 April' and this date would have a red dot on it.

For the travel agency the planner could show:

- 'Complete and check invitation list for mail shot: 1 December' with a blue star on the date.

Better still, use your diary to note the dates for completing key activities. By first logging the 'end dates', work backwards and enter various intermediate time schedules by which all the subsidiary tasks require to be completed. This means that if the entry for Monday 20 January states:

– 'Should have completed outline'

and it is not quite finished, the deadline can either be moved forward by a few days (provided sufficient flexibility was allowed in the plan), or midnight oil has to be burned to complete the work on time.

A typical diary page for either entrepreneur might show:

For the author:

10 April:

- Library – lunch-time.
- Visit local bookshop – late night opening (10 p.m.)
- Should have a shortlist of publishers by now.
- Weekly Director's Meeting.
- Lisa's birthday Friday – book table/order roses.

For the travel agency:

1 December:

- Colour leaflets for cruise promotion should have arrived.
- Confirm venue booking for 31 January.
- Complete invitation list by now.

Because you use your diary every day to view and review commitments of every sort, it is the one reminder system that is pretty well foolproof in ensuring that your plans are progressing – as planned.

Coping with Contingencies

Making plans is one thing. Ensuring that they work out as you planned is another. Things can happen which are not under your control. In order to combat unforeseen problems, you need to:

- Build in a certain amount of flexibility to your time schedules.

- Make provisions to cope with emergencies.

For example: the author may lose a week's work because of a faulty disk (and need to resolve to make back-up copies to ensure this does not happen again); the travel agency may face an unexpected increase in the price of wine (and have to approach a cruise company to share the costs and meet the shortfall).

In both cases, there is a need to ensure that some form of contingency plans exist, otherwise, when something drastic occurs, there is a temptation to give up the plan altogether, rather than adapt it to suit changes of circumstance.

Not everything you want to achieve is achieved smoothly. People who may not be directly part of the plan may have an influence on how the plan progresses.

For the author:

It is vital to set time aside to write and re-write his/her magnum opus, while for the spouse, enjoying an active social life may be a main interest. It is important that their different needs are accommodated, and this may mean setting additional time aside in order to go out together.

For the travel agency:

The preferred venue for the promotion could prove to be fully booked for the foreseeable future. This means an alternative location has to be found.

It is vital to be flexible enough to change and amend the plan when circumstances dictate.

Taking Remedial Action

If you find that your progress is not as good as you were aiming for, you need to take remedial action very promptly, or your plan could go badly awry.

It is no good thinking that if you ignore problems they will go away. Usually they get worse, unless something positive is done to solve them.

For example, if the author finds there are a great many publishers who publish the sort of literature he or she wants to write, might it be better to concentrate on finding an agent who would channel it in the right direction?

Or if the travel agency finds, when going through existing customer records, that very few clients in the area went on cruises in the last two years, is this the best product to promote? Especially if, while doing this research, it becomes apparent that there is a huge market for family holidays in Spain.

For various aspects of your plan, it may be necessary to go back to the drawing board because what seemed a fruitful course of action did not work out as planned.

Keeping Control

By identifying the actions required, the schedule to be followed and the expected costs, you have laid down the standards which require to be met and which will indicate successful performance.

For planning to be effective, controlling progress must be an integral part of the process. It is no good starting a journey with high hopes, only to find that you lose your way and you have no method of knowing where you are or how to get yourself back on course.

Ensuring that you know how things are progressing is a vital component in keeping your plan on track and requires as much energy and attention as setting up the plan in the first place.

Summary: Getting There

Just because you have committed your plan to paper does not mean it will happen. Managing and monitoring the plan requires your continuous interest.

You need to be clear what has to be done and to co-ordinate what is happening, especially if others are involved. If you can cope with contingencies or even anticipate problems before they arise, you will be going a long way to make sure that things are staying on track. Taking immediate remedial action is the key should something not go as planned.

Implementing the plan requires constant effort, vigilance and commitment. While carrying out the plan you may need to remind yourself from time to time of the final destination – your ultimate aim.

Questions to Ask Yourself

Think about how you keep your plan on track and answer the following questions:

➤ Do I have a system for keeping tabs on my plan?

➤ Am I keeping within the time-scales and financial limits I set?

➤ Have I worked out how I could deal with delays or unforeseen problems?

➤ Do I know if things are going according to plan?

You Will Be Doing Better If...

★ You check your actions against your plan.

★ You use your systems to keep track of progress.

★ You stay within your budget.

★ You allow enough time in your timetable.

★ You think about how you might cope with contingencies.

★ You can clearly see how the plan is progressing.

6.   Measuring Success

The final and most important step in the process of planning is to measure the success of your plan by examining how well you have achieved your objectives ('How do I know that I've got there?').

As well as knowing how well you performed your key activities, you also need to evaluate whether the plan was in line with your ultimate aim.

Judging Performance

To judge your efficiency you have to measure what actually happened against what was planned. In this way, if things do not go as well as expected you know what went wrong and why.

The process involves measuring:

- **The quality**, or **the consistency**, of the work: whether it is equal to what was planned, or not.

- **The quantity** or **the amount** of work: whether it is more, or less, than was planned.

- **The time-scale** in which the work was required to be completed. This is the one thing you are likely to be well-aware of if all has not gone according to plan.

- **The real cost** against the predicted costs. With good planning, these will not be far apart.

For the author the thorough research, well-presented letter and excellent outline (*quality*) submitted to six chosen publishers resulted in four rejections, one no-reply, and one expression of interest (*quantity*) in the idea but suggesting a complete reworking of the text. The whole procedure took longer than planned (*time-scale*) because replies were so slow and endless chivvying was necessary. This incurred extra expense as there were many more telephone calls and letters involved (*real cost*) than estimated.

For the travel agency the cocktail party was much enjoyed with excellent eats and wine (*quality*); 30 people arrived which was 50% more than accepted the invitation (*quantity*). This meant that it was more expensive than planned (*real-cost*), but two people made a booking on the evening itself and another four booked the following week (*time-scale*).

Evaluating Your Effort

Evaluating your plan helps you to decide what to do next. You have to decide whether your plan was effective, and if so, whether you will do it again or do it differently. Take as objective a view as you can.

The effort you put in and the results you get out are not always equal. You may find that very little is achieved from a huge amount of effort. This means you need to take stock and decide what part of the plan needs radical revision.

But you also need to bear in mind that the results may have been affected by outside influences – things which could have modified the outcome of all your efforts and which were nothing to do with your plan.

Conversely, for very little effort on your part the results may be quite spectacular. This may be because you did exactly the right things at the right time as you were in touch with what was needed. Or it could be that external factors were enhancing the results.

Evaluating the author's plan:

The initial results for the author were disappointing. Despite a great deal of carefully planned effort, there was little reward. This was due, in part, to the author's unfamiliarity with the publishing world. During this phase of the plan, experience and knowledge was acquired as to how to approach things more effectively.

The author decides not to repeat that part of the plan which relates to finding a suitable publisher, but to try to find an agent instead, and builds a large contingency factor into the estimated costs.

Evaluating the travel agency's plan:

The travel agency achieved much more than expected. They had targeted the right market. But their efforts were aided by the fact that the weather had been appalling for the previous month and people were desperate to have something wonderful to look forward to. While they achieved more than their minimum requirement of bookings, they also need to be aware of the part external factors played in their success.

The travel agency decide to capitalize on their success and to specialize in cruises which the more affluent newcomers to town are prepared to buy. They now want to increase their reputation for quality service – which means making another plan.

Summary: How I Know I Am There

Once you have measured and evaluated the results of your plan, you are in a position to judge if what you have achieved was worth the effort.

Planning is a continuous activity which needs to go on all the time if you are to achieve anything. By knowing where you are now and keeping your ultimate aim in mind, you can decide where you next want to be and work out a further plan of action.

So get stuck in and start another one.

Questions to Ask Yourself

To judge the success of your plan, you need to answer the following questions:

➤ Was the quality achieved what I expected?

➤ Was the quantity sufficient?

➤ Were the costs within the budget?

➤ Was the plan completed on time?

➤ Would more effort have achieved better results?

➤ Was the plan sensible?

➤ Was the plan worthwhile?

Your answers to these questions will either help you make adjustments to ensure things work out as planned next time, or they will enable you to feel very pleased with yourself.

You Will Be Doing Better If...

★ You measure your actual performance against your planned performance.

★ You evaluate the results.

★ You understand the importance of planning.

★ You feel you are well on the way to becoming a confident and effective planner.

★ You are now ready to develop further plans.

★ You are considerably closer to achieving your ultimate aim.

Check List for Planning

If your plan does not quite work out as anticipated, it is unlikely that fault will be found with the whole plan. It is more likely due to one specific area not being quite right. The root causes of the problem could be:

Knowing Your Starting Point

It may be that you did not get (or were not given) the correct facts, or that you did not accurately assess what was needed. If you did not obtain accurate information, evaluate the current situation, or identify your opportunities, you may have built your plan on quicksand. The amount of initial preparation you carry out before you start is the most critical factor in the overall success of the plan.

Setting Goals

If you find that at some point you have deviated from your original goal, it may be that you did not set course in the right direction at the outset. If you have not correctly identified your purpose, or kept that goal in sight at every stage of planning, then your key activities may well be misconceived and you could find yourself heading in the wrong direction.

Monitoring Your Plans

If your monitoring process has not been correctly set up, you will not be able to check which parts of the plan are working or even which are working better than others. As the effort you put into achieving your key activities is the essence of making your plan work, it is important to keep close track of progress. Remember, not all effort produces the desired results. This is why an effective monitoring system is the backbone of planning.

Scheduling Activities

If 'not having enough time' has been a cause for concern, make sure you build extra hours, days, or weeks, into your timetable. The amount of time allowed for each stage of your plan must be sufficient.

Achieving Results

If your plan did not produce what you expected, you need to know how and where there is room for improvement. You will not be able to judge the full effect of your plan unless you take the trouble to measure the outcome of your efforts. This allows you to make adjustments to any further plans. It also goes a long way to guarantee future success.

The Benefits of Planning

Planning is an integral part of work, not an optional extra to be used for special occasions.

Formulating a plan does not have to take an enormous effort, nor need the prospect of planning be so daunting that you never get started.

The benefits of planning are that:

- You will become clear about your ultimate aims.

- You will have confidence that your day-to-day action is purposeful.

- You will be able to analyse objectively.

- You will be more methodical in your thinking.

- You will be able to capitalize on the strong points of your business or profession.

- You will minimize the weak spots.

- You will get things done.

Glossary

Here are some definitions in relation to Planning.

Action – Purposeful movement which requires effort, the only way to achieve aims and objectives.

Commitment – Carrying out the act long after the mood has left you.

Control – The exercise of personal influence required to ensure that things are working out the way they were planned.

Cost – Expenditure essential to carrying out the plan.

Intentions – What your mind is paved with. In an ideal world you would translate them all into action.

Key activities – Imperative areas of action.

Measurement – Objective assessment of results.

Movement – Purposeless activity which gives the rest of the world the impression you are doing something.

Opportunities – Likely openings which need to be identified.

Organizing – Taking necessary action and being prepared.

Planning – Bringing ideas to fruition by design rather than by chance.

Quality – Standard of excellence which meets all expectations.

Resources – Items which should be brought to the aid of all plans. Rarely used to best advantage.

Strong Points – Advantages which form the foundation from which to develop your plan.

Standards – Yardsticks against which to measure performance.

System – A simple method for tracking your progress on a day-to-day basis, e.g. a diary.

Time-scale – Pace and duration of a plan. Accurate estimates of this are vital to its success.

Threats – Hidden menaces which need to be over-come, at least in spirit.

Weak Spots – Defects which can prevent you from getting your plan off the ground.

Jargon

There are a number of popular jargon terms which crop up in relation to planning:

Critical Path Analysis – A fancy way of monitoring your plan's progress.

Mission – A bland statement of business aims, usually compiled by committee with the lack of clarity attendant upon such decisions.

PERT – Programme Evaluation Review Technique; an acronym for keeping track of progress.

SWOT – Strengths, Weaknesses, Opportunities, Threats; an acronym for the snapshot test.

Vision – The brainchild of one person, usually in need of heavenly aid.

The Author

Kate Keenan is a Chartered Occupational Psychologist with degrees in affiliated subjects (B.Sc., M.Phil.) and a number of qualifications in others.

She founded Keenan Research, an industrial psychology consultancy, in 1978. The work of the consultancy is fundamentally concerned with helping people to achieve their potential and make a better job of their management.

By devising work programmes for companies she enables them to target and remedy their managerial problems – from personnel selection and individual assessment to team building and attitude surveys. She believes in giving priority to training the managers to institute their own programmes, so that their company resources are developed and expanded.

Convinced that planning plays a central part in successful management, she is well aware that putting good intentions to work is a disciplined, but rewarding, process. So much so, that she now makes plans for the fun of it.

THE MANAGEMENT GUIDES

Available now at £2.99 each:

Making Time ☐

Managing ☐

Managing Yourself ☐

Planning ☐

Selecting People ☐

Solving Problems ☐

To be published in July 1995:

Communicating ☐

Delegating ☐

Meetings ☐

Motivating ☐

Negotiating ☐

Understanding Behaviour ☐